Williams have gotten out of men's clothes and into the act in a number of recent films.

A few performers have gone beyond burlesque, of course, and the on-screen and off-screen androgyny of Marlene Dietrich and Greta Garbo, David Bowie and Tim Curry have ultimately crossed the line between fantasy and reality, dictating fashion trends and changing forever our preconceived notions about men and women and sex roles in general.

Today, the door of the collective Hollywood closet has swung open all the way. Real-life female impersonator Divine scored mainstream hits (*Polyester, Hairspray*) in the last decade, and the world of the drag performer was big-box-office fodder for *Victor/Victoria* and *La Cage aux Folles*. More recently, Jaye Davidson was nominated for an Academy Award for his/her surprising performance in the gender-bending blockbuster *The Crying Game*.

Times have changed, of course, but humor hasn't. It is reassuring to know that as long as there are comedians like Martin and Williams, there will probably always be room for a pie in someone's face and a man masquerading in mascara.

Cary Grant

I WAS A MALE WAR BRIDE, 1949

*The English-born actor with the London-meets-Hollywood accent
makes an unbelievable Frenchman and an even more
unlikely woman in this outrageous comedy of errors directed by
Howard Hawks. Trying to beat the bureaucracy and follow his
American-army-lieutenant wife (Ann Sheridan) back to the U.S.,
the priggish Grant is eventually forced to don women's clothes in
one scene in this subversively funny picture, described by a critic
at the time as "not likely to appeal to prudish audiences."*

Sydney Chaplin
CHARLEY'S AUNT, 1925 (ABOVE)

Although not as successful as younger brother Charles, the former hard-luck London vagabond shone briefly on the silver screen as the homely but hilarious Aunt Babbs in this adaptation of the beloved Victorian stage farce. Remade in 1930, the film is best remembered in its third incarnation, starring drag hall-of-famer Jack Benny.

Tony Curtis
SOME LIKE IT HOT, 1959 (RIGHT)

One of the most celebrated tributes to transvestism ever committed to celluloid, this Billy Wilder-directed farce featured enough high-speed slapstick and role confusion to deflect just how unbelievable (and unattractive!) Curtis and Jack Lemmon were playing two women. Not a pleasant experience for the tough-guy actor (his drag voice had to be dubbed), the picture was one high-camp spectacle that rose above bad taste.

SL(UA)P-14

Tim Curry

THE ROCKY HORROR PICTURE SHOW,
1975

*Sweet success finally came to the
"sweet transvestite from Transylvania" only after
this comedy-horror-musical finally caught on
with teen audiences on the midnight-movie-house
circuit. The very definition of a cult film,
the bizarre tale of sex, cannibalism (Meatloaf,
appropriately, is eaten), murder, and more sex is
still a rite of passage for many young moviegoers,
whose audience participation (and the charismatic
performance by Curry) is perhaps the most
fascinating thing about this low-budget remake
of the British stage play by the same name.*

Divine (with Susan Walsh and Cookie Mueller)

FEMALE TROUBLE, 1974

Flash/trash director John Waters sank
to new depths of high camp in this cult classic,
which follows the life of loving mother,
model, and mass murderer Dawn Davenport,
played by the overweight and over-the-top
Harris Glenn Milstead, aka Divine.
Notorious for his/her role as "the filthiest person
alive" in Waters's previous Pink Flamingos
and later a mainstream hit in Hairspray,
the real-life transvestite and glamour-girl-
wannabe literally tops herself in one infamous
sex scene in this outrageous look at the downside
(and backside) of the American dream.

Hanns Lothar
ONE, TWO, THREE, 1961
This fast and furious Ninotchka-*like farce, shot on location in Berlin and called by* Time *magazine a "bewildered but wonderfully funny exercise in nonstop nuttiness," earned no Oscars (and few box-office receipts) for director Billy Wilder or star James Cagney (his last movie for twenty years). The film did feature, however, one of Wilder's improbable yet funny drag routines à la* Some Like It Hot: *even Jack Lemmon looked better in high heels and hat than this decidedly unfeminine would-be fräulein!*

14

Danny Kaye

ON THE DOUBLE, 1961 (ABOVE)

Playing a dual role as he had earlier in On the Riviera,
the former Borscht-Belt comedian born Daniel Kaminski is an
American private forced to impersonate an English officer in this
zany spoof of the spy film genre. Although he manages to fool British
intelligence, the star misses the mark in his impersonation of the
great Marlene Dietrich, whose voice was lower, legs longer,
and who certainly didn't sport a mustache!

Charlie Chaplin

A WOMAN, 1915 (RIGHT)

Chaplin once remarked that all he needed to make a great comedy
was "a park, a policeman, and a pretty girl." He played the
pretty girl himself in this two-reeler from Essanay Studios,
where the former London street waif soon commanded $10,000
per week as Hollywood's richest "Little Tramp."

Boris Karloff

THE GIRL FROM U.N.C.L.E., 1966

*The sinister English-born actor who became the world's most
infamous movie monster in the original* Frankenstein *surfaced
as a very different type of monster in this spin-off of the popular
"Man From U.N.C.L.E." television series. As the satanic
"Mother Muffin" who locks horns with the show's star, Stephanie
Powers, the bewigged seventy-nine-year-old one-man
(-woman) horror show would have frightened even his own
original monster thirty-five years earlier.*

Rod Steiger

No Way To Treat a Lady, 1967

*A master of disguises with a mother fixation and drag routine to rival
Norman Bates's, Steiger is funny and horrific all at once as a
charming Boston-Strangler-type serial killer, whose calling card is the
bright-red lipstick marks he leaves on his victims' necks. One of
Hollywood's most accomplished screen villains, the Oscar-winning
method actor makes an equally effective villainess in this comedy-
cum-murder mystery based on the novel by William Goldman.*

Robin Williams
Mrs. Doubtfire, 1993

That manic man of a thousand faces (and voices) is one hell of an old lady in this Twentieth Century-Fox comedy that is nothing less than a showcase for its (fe)male lead. Done up as a fussy English nanny named Euphegenia Doubtfire so he can see his children by his estranged wife (Sally Field), Williams follows in the footsteps of legendary high-heelers Jack Benny and Milton Berle, offering up a string of virtuoso performances (dancing with a vacuum cleaner when no one is looking, protecting himself from the advances of an elderly bus driver) that masks the highly improbable plot of this Mary Poppins-*meets*-Charley's Aunt *crowd-pleaser.*

Preston Foster
Up the River, 1938
*Was there ever an unlikelier dame than the burly,
six-feet-two-inch, 200-pound former pro wrestler and he-man star
of over a hundred Hollywood actioners? Playing an ex-convict trying
to escape the heat in this remake of the 1930 original starring
Spencer Tracy, Foster should get twenty to life
(in the women's pen!) for his fake blonde locks and girlie getup.*

William Powell

LOVE CRAZY, 1941

*All hell breaks loose when Powell feigns insanity to prevent his wife
from divorcing him in this zany comedy of errors. Paired for the tenth
time with his on-screen wife and sometime-combatant Myrna Loy,
the dapper MGM star stops chasing skirts and puts one on
(and shaves his trademark mustache as well) in order to escape the
nuthouse where he was placed by the authorities. Fooling the world
(but not his wife, who now wants him back), Powell eventually joins
Loy in their bedroom at the film's close (still dressed in drag!),
as her meddling mother bids them both to "sleep well."*

Steve Martin
DEAD MEN DON'T WEAR PLAID, 1982 (ABOVE)

*Mostly an exercise in clever editing, this largely sophomoric tribute
to film noir pits its star against the likes of James Cagney,
Ava Gardner, and Bogie and Bacall. Beyond the cleverly manipulated
clips from such classic 1940s fare as* White Heat *and* The Killers,
*the film is most interesting for the occasional clever one-liner
and Martin's hilarious but unlikely transformation in one
scene into a Barbara Stanwyck-like femme fatale.*

Dustin Hoffman (with Sydney Pollack)
TOOTSIE, 1982 (RIGHT)

*Hardly a believable woman (much less a <u>Southern</u> woman),
Hoffman does his best in this incredibly popular sitcom-like story
of an out-of-work actor who will do anything to get a job.
One joke taken a bit too seriously, the film would have really
soared with a lighter touch. Paging Billy Wilder . . .*

Paul Lynde (with Eric Fleming)
THE GLASS BOTTOM BOAT, 1966
*The wisecracking, cynical star of the stage and screen versions of
Bye Bye Birdie and for years the quipping center square on the
"Hollywood Squares" game show, Lynde hammed it up per usual
as a flustered security guard posing as a woman in this frantic spy
spoof-cum-romantic comedy from MGM. With Technicolor-red hair
piled higher than costar Doris Day's, the eternally exasperated
comedian with the funny voice looked like the proverbial carping
mother-in-law we wished we never had.*

Jack Benny (with Laird Cregar)

CHARLEY'S AUNT, 1941

*The would-be concert violinist and former radio star born
Benjamin Kubelsky made this time-worn Victorian chestnut
(the movie and the character!) an instant classic, playing the nutty
Aunt Babbs from Brazil. With his perfect comic timing and famously
light step, Benny was the most believable—albeit none-too-beautiful—
of the "women" to play the title role in this third of four
film versions of the popular British stage farce.*

Jerry Lewis (with Mike Kellin and Dewey Robinson)
AT WAR WITH THE ARMY, 1951
Featuring an old-fashioned drag vignette straight from the
pie-in-your-face school of vaudeville comedy, this mildly amusing
military farce is most remarkable as the first star vehicle for Lewis
and Dean Martin, who would go on to make fifteen more pictures
together in just five years—all smash hits. The goofball comedian's
hairy chest and bushy eyebrows notwithstanding, at least one
GI Joe finds Lewis appealing in a blonde wig and low-cut blouse.
The war must have been longer than we thought!

George Sanders
THE KREMLIN LETTER, 1970

This star-studded cold-war spy thriller directed by John Huston featured one of Hollywood's suavest scoundrels in one of his last—and unlikeliest—roles. When the Oscar-winning star of All About Eve *and author of* Memoirs of a Professional Cad *donned a blonde wig and glamorous feathered boa as The Warlock, a professional female impersonator, for one cameo scene in this black suspense comedy, aging Russian-born, English-reared actor looked more like his two previous wives, Zsa Zsa and Magda Gabor, than a debonair leading man. Bored with life, his career on the skids, Sanders committed suicide two years later.*

Tony Curtis and Jack Lemmon (with Joe E. Brown, right)
SOME LIKE IT HOT, 1959

*Only director Billy Wilder could have elevated an improbable story
with bad taste galore into high art. Maybe the best authentic
depiction of the Roaring Twenties ever committed to film,
the Oscar-nominated blockbuster features Curtis and Lemmon
as two musicians in drag who must fend off the mob as well as the
amorous advances of every oversexed man from Chicago to Miami.
As the wacky tycoon Osgood E. Fielding III, Brown finally discovers
that his fiancée is a he, not a she. His response, "Nobody's perfect,"
may be the funniest tag line in Hollywood history.*

Joe E. Brown
SHUT MY BIG MOUTH, 1942 (ABOVE)
The one-time vaudeville star brought his big mouth and low-brow
slapstick style to a number of small-budget Hollywood farces in the
1930s and 1940s. Having camped it up in his previous picture,
So You Won't Talk, *Brown goes one step further dressed in drag to*
escape a gang of outlaws in this show-stopping, ear-popping scene.

Jerry Lewis
SCARED STIFF, 1953 (LEFT)
Promoted appropriately with the line "They're making a spook-tacle
of themselves," this particularly nutty installment in the Lewis-
Martin comedy cycle featured one of Tinseltown's classic show-within-
the-movie female impersonations. Visiting a girl (Lizabeth Scott) who
has inherited a haunted castle off the coast of Cuba in this remake of
the 1940 Bob Hope vehicle, Lewis is an even fruitier cha-cha queen
than his banana-brained costar Carmen Miranda.

Mickey Rooney
BABES ON BROADWAY, 1941

The best of the Busby Berkeley musicals starring Rooney and Judy Garland, this sequel to the popular Babes in Arms *made its stars MGM's number-one box-office draws. Demonstrating a brilliant talent for impersonation when he imitates a host of past theatrical entertainers, the pint-size dynamo with a predilection for tall, glamorous women (he's been married to eight, including screen sirens Ava Gardner and Martha Vickers) shines as one himself in eight-inch heels and gold lamé as Brazilian bombshell Carmen Miranda.*

Stan Laurel and Oliver Hardy

THAT'S MY WIFE, 1929

The most successful comedy team of all time gets into "another fine mess"
when Laurel dresses up as Hardy's wife to impress his rich uncle in this
two-reel silent directed by Hal Roach. Married on-camera once more
fourteen years later in Jitterbugs, *the celluloid couple were closer in real*
life than many husbands and wives, and neither ever married. Inconsolable
after Hardy's death in 1957, Laurel retired from the screen forever.

Red Skelton

BATHING BEAUTY, 1944

*Esther Williams's first starring vehicle featured more of
the red-headed one-time vaudeville performer in drag than the
star in bathing suits! An over-the-top (even for MGM) series
of waterlogged vignettes, the film is more interesting for the
high-camp hilarity of the aqua-ballet finale than for Skelton's
low-camp washout in ballet slippers and tutu.*

Lou Costello (with Bud Abbott)

LOST IN A HAREM, 1944

One of the earliest celluloid pairings of Abbott and Costello,
this uproariously funny MGM farce was also one of the duo's best.
Dressed incredibly as a harem girl (and hypnotized to boot!),
the portly half of the celebrated comedy team fights off the advances of
a conniving sultan as well as assorted Arabs from Casablanca to
Timbuktu. A smash hit, the picture helped make the zany pair
one of Hollywood's top-ten box-office draws until 1952.

The Three Stooges
WEE, WEE MONSIEUR, 1938 (ABOVE)

*The head-bopping, eye-gouging, nose-tweaking trio should have
been renamed "The Three Stoogettes" for this typically cartoon-like
two-reeler. Although the long-running comedy team specializing in
violent, vulgar slapstick never made much money for Columbia
Pictures, Moe (Moses Horowitz) Larry (Lawrence Feinberg), and
Curly (Jerome Horowitz) enjoyed more fame when their nearly 200
comedy shorts were shown on television beginning in the late 1950s.*

Eddie Cantor (with Alan Rinehart)
ALI BABA GOES TO TOWN, 1937 (RIGHT)

*The pop-eyed vaudeville star born Edward Isadore Izkowitz plays a
hobo who falls off a train into an Arabian Nights movie set he thinks
is the real thing in this musical comedy full of dual roles and double
meanings. The obligatory drag scene (with Cantor a surprisingly
pretty harem girl) and musical numbers aside, the film is really
a well-disguised but wry political commentary blasting
New Deal policies at home and fascism abroad.*

Harpo and Chico Marx
A NIGHT AT THE OPERA, 1935 (PAGES 46-47)

*Those masters of mass hysteria take on high society in the comedy
team's most famous picture, their first for MGM and one of
Hollywood's most hilarious. When the brothers bring the house down
(literally) dressed in drag as Italian opera singers during a production
of "Il Trovatore," the audience on-screen and off has never had
a better time. Prima donnas in real life as well, the notoriously
difficult Groucho, Chico, and Harpo finally went their separate ways
(Zeppo had cut out in 1933) after making* Love Happy,
their final film together, in 1950.

Bob Hope (with Walter Brennan)
THE PRINCESS AND THE PIRATE, 1944 (RIGHT)

*The wisecracking one-time vaudeville star and future American
institution is on the run from a power-mad potentate in this typically
wacky travel adventure-cum-musical comedy from Samuel Goldwyn.
The only thing more amusing than Hope's impersonation of a crazy
gypsy woman is Brennan's out-of-character turn as an even crazier
pirate. Everyone's favorite comic coward, Hope eventually faces
the enemy, becoming a man again (in more ways than one!)
and getting the girl (Virginia Mayo) by the film's end.*

John Hansen
THE CHRISTINE JORGENSEN STORY, 1970 (PAGES 50-51)

*A pre-tabloid-TV celluloid shocker, the tale of real-life
Christine Jorgensen is noteworthy only as the first Hollywood film
to address the taboo subject of transsexuality. Taking drag one step
further in this low-budget, high-camp biopic, the title character is
transformed into an anatomically correct woman by the film's end.
The only problem is that pretty-boy Hansen somehow looks
more masculine after the big switch than before!*

Bob Hope and Joan Fontaine

CASANOVA'S BIG NIGHT, 1954

*Starring in the last of his big-budget burlesque comedies,
Hope is masquerading as Casanova this time around, fleeing creditors
from Venice to Vesuvius in a wild array of typically outlandish getups.
Most amusing for its all-star cast (everyone from Lon Chaney, Jr.
to Vincent Price), the costume extravaganza is also notable for the
double-delight drag turn of Hope and his mustachioed costar Fontaine
as Venetian courtiers who rock a few gondolas in one outrageous scene.*

Julie Andrews (with James Garner)

Victor/Victoria, 1982

Although Andrews looks great in a Berlin Bowie tux, this topsy-turvy tale of sexual ambivalence based on the 1933 German film Viktor und Viktoria *is a bit of a stretch for the wholesome star of such saccharine fare as* Mary Poppins *and* The Sound of Music. *Bringing little of an impersonator's hauteur to her complicated role as a woman who falls in love with a man (Garner) who thinks she is a* he *(whew!), the square-jawed actress is perhaps most handsome as a man when all is said and done. Directed by the star's husband, Blake Edwards, the madcap musical did manage to challenge quite a few preconceived notions about gender and sexuality, as well as pick up Oscars for Best Score and Adaptation.*

Barbra Streisand (with Amy Irving)

YENTL, 1983

*The megalomaniacal and multi-talented Oscar, Emmy, and
Tony winner tries her hand at directing (as well as starring in)
this musical version of the Isaac Bashevis Singer short story about a
young woman who poses as a man so she can study the Torah.
Streisand is credible enough in a male role, even when belting out
the show tunes that string the movie's disparate scenes together.
Really a classic tale of mistaken identity, the picture has a few funny
moments, especially when Hadass (Irving) finally insists on consum-
mating her marriage to the understandably reluctant Yentl.*

Elizabeth Taylor (with Mickey Rooney)
NATIONAL VELVET, 1944 (RIGHT)
Remember when Elizabeth Taylor was young, innocent, and
adorable? The twelve-year-old, violet-eyed Hollywood princess almost
steals the show (Shirley Temple turned down the role) in this three-
handkerchief MGM classic, whose real star is a horse named "Pie."
Not yet the well-built love goddess and much-married
scene-stealer/maker she would later become, Taylor is almost
believable masquerading as a boy in order to ride her stallion
to victory in the Grand National Steeplechase.

Joyce Hyser (with Toni Hudson)
JUST ONE OF THE GUYS, 1985 (PAGES 60-61)
A sort of Tootsie-*in-reverse, this surprisingly well done teen-lust*
comedy-with-a-message features an unknown but engaging cast that
aims to please. When Hyser disguises herself as a boy in order to be
taken more seriously by her teachers and win a journalism prize, sex
roles, teen roles, and the high school itself are all turned upside down.

Annabella (with Henry Fonda)
WINGS OF THE MORNING, 1937 (ABOVE)

*This slight tale of Irish gypsies, horse racing, and mistaken identity
is as full of blarney as the Blarney Stone itself. Featuring the French
actress born Suzanne Charpentier (the future Mrs. Tyrone Power)
and a very young Henry Fonda, the far-fetched romantic comedy is
most memorable for its leading lady's drag turn as leading man and
the early Technicolor hues of the Killarney landscapes.*

Miriam Hopkins (with Kitty Carlisle)
SHE LOVES ME NOT, 1934 (LEFT)

*This larky romantic farce was remade two more times—
in 1942 and 1955. Showcasing the considerable talents of its former
chorus-girl star as a woman on the lam posing as a student in a male
college, this decidedly superior version is short on believability
(Hopkins's lipstick and eyeshadow would have given her away)
but long on clever dialogue and catchy tunes by Bing Crosby.*

Louise Brooks (with Richard Arlen)

BEGGARS OF LIFE, 1928

*For years one of Hollywood's most enigmatic recluses, the temperamental star
of a handful of 1920s silents gives a haunting portrayal of a woman gone wrong
in this cult classic from director William Wellman. Murdering her father,
who had tried to rape her, and then donning men's clothes (in one of filmdom's
earliest instances of male drag) to seek refuge with a group of hobos, the twenty-
two-year old gives a performance that would help land her her most famous role
as the sex-obsessed Lulu in the German production of* Pandora's Box. *After
making a few more critically acclaimed films in Europe, Brooks eventually
returned to Hollywood, briefly earning a living as a nightclub dancer and
bit player in B westerns before retiring from the screen forever.*

Greta Garbo (with John Gilbert, center)
QUEEN CHRISTINA, 1933
Although she could never be mistaken for a man, the screen's most celebrated beauty played on her own (and the historical Queen Christina's) androgyny in the most famous role reversal ever committed to film. Distressed at the thought of a political marriage, the seventeenth-century queen of Sweden wanders her country dressed in men's clothing, eventually falling in love with the Spanish ambassador, played by Garbo's real-life ex-lover Gilbert. The legendary Swedish-born actress was said to have identified closely with her country's former monarch, who had a distaste for men (and marriage) and who eventually abdicated the throne to live out her final years alone in Rome. Life imitated art when Hollywood's own queen abdicated eight years after the release of the MGM classic.

Katharine Hepburn
SYLVIA SCARLETT, 1935
(RIGHT AND PAGES 70-71, WITH BRIAN AHERNE)
Called by one critic "a tragic waste of time and screen talent,"
this daring but admittedly confusing tale was loathed by audiences
at the time, as well as by the star herself. Today a cult favorite,
the George Cukor-directed comedy-adventure costarring
Cary Grant is adored by Hepburn-Grant enthusiasts
(it was their first picture together), as well as feminists and lesbians,
who appreciate the independent actress's uncompromisingly
realistic portrayal of the opposite sex.

Marlene Dietrich (with Paul Porcasi)
MOROCCO, 1930 (LEFT)

*In top hat and tails, the glamorous German star capitalized
on the tradition of "La Garçonne," the boy/girl conundrum
that Paris and Berlin found so intriguing between the wars.
When Dietrich sang in her husky voice "What Am I Bid
for My Apples?" and then kissed a woman on the mouth in
the outrageous opening scene of* Morocco, *audiences were
introduced to a new kind of continental vamp—
androgynous, like Garbo, but far from suffering.
Playing on her mysterious sexuality throughout her career,
the Teutonic temptress donned male attire on-screen
as well as off (creating a fashion sensation),
especially during her second run as a sold-out concert
performer in the 1960s and 1970s.*

PETER PAN (PARAMOUNT PICTURES), 1920S
(PAGES 74-75)

*This silent short based on the classic J. M. Barrie play
about a boy who refuses to grow up featured a young girl in
the title role, one of the few instances of a child playing the
opposite sex in a Hollywood picture. It was the last movie
adaptation of the tale (Disney did an animated version in
1953) until a much older woman (Mary Martin) reprised
her beloved stage role for film some forty years later.*

@·D·1011·K·220

Merle Oberon

A SONG TO REMEMBER, 1945

The exotically beautiful half-Indian, Tasmanian-born Oberon was perhaps a bit too glamorous in her role as the infamous nineteenth-century French novelist George Sand (née Amandine Dupin), who adopted male attire and a man's name after divorcing her aristocratic first husband. A wildly inaccurate Hollywood biopic, the film did capture the rebellious spirit of its sexually ambiguous hero/heroine, whose affair with composer Frederic Chopin (played by Cornel Wilde) is one of the world's great—and most unusual—love stories.

Julie Andrews
Victor/Victoria, 1982

CREDITS AND SOURCES

TEXT: J. SPENCER BECK

DESIGN: LISA LYTTON-SMITH
PHOTO EDITOR: LESLIE FRATKIN

Front Cover: Archive Photos
3: Everett Collection
7: Courtesy The Kobal Collection
8: Everett Collection
9: Everett Collection
10-11: Photofest
12-13: Photofest
15: Lester Glassner Collection/Neal Peters
16: Lester Glassner Collection/Neal Peters
17: Culver Pictures
18: Lester Glassner Collection/Neal Peters
19: Lester Glassner Collection/Neal Peters
20: Neal Peters Collection
21: Courtesy Twentieth Century-Fox
22: Everett Collection
23: Lester Glassner Collection/Neal Peters
24: Lester Glassner Collection/Neal Peters
25: Everett Collection
26: Lester Glassner Collection/ Neal Peters
27: Courtesy The Kobal Collection
29: Photofest
30-31: Photofest
32: Archive Photos
33: Culver Pictures
34: Lester Glassner Collection/Neal Peters
35: Lester Glassner Collection/Neal Peters

37: Courtesy The Kobal Collection
38: Photofest
40: Courtesy The Kobal Collection
43: Everett Collection
44: Neal Peters Collection
45: Everett Collection
46-47: Everett Collection
49: Lester Glassner Collection/Neal Peters
50-51: Everett Collection
53: Culver Pictures
54-55: Lester Glassner Collection/Neal Peters
56: Neal Peters Collection
58: Archive Photos
60-61: Everett Collection
62: Culver Pictures
63: Lester Glassner Collection/Neal Peters
64: Photofest
66-67: Photofest
68: Photofest
70-71: Photofest
72-73: Lester Glassner Collection/Neal Peters
74-75: Photofest
76: Courtesy The Kobal Collection
78: Everett Collection
Back Cover: Everett Collection

HOLLYWOOD

DRAG

EDITED BY J.C. SUARÈS

THOMASSON-GRANT